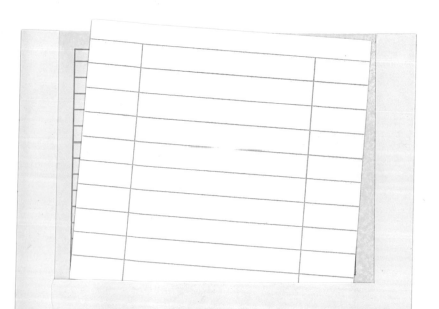

# USE
# COMPUTERS AS
# A RESOURCE

# Richard A. Diem

A Social Studies Skills Book
FRANKLIN WATTS/1983
New York/Toronto/London/Sydney

Photographs courtesy of
Commodore Business Machines: p. 4;
IBM: pp. 12, 14, 25, 43, 50, 59;
Tandy Corp,/Radio Shack: p. 54;
Control Data Corp.; pp. 67, 76.

Diagrams courtesy of Vantage Art, Inc.

Library of Congress Cataloging in Publication Data

Diem, Richard A.
How to use computers as a resource.

(A Social studies skill book)
Bibliography: p.
Includes index.
Summary: Describes the vocabulary of computer
technology and ways of computing from the abacus to
the microcomputer; discusses solving problems with
computers and using computers in the social sciences and
in classroom social studies; and projects the future of
computers.
1. Social sciences—Data processing—Juvenile
literature.    2. Social sciences—Study and teaching—
Data processing—Juvenile literature.    [1. Social
sciences—Data processing.    2. Data processing.
3. Computers]    I. Title.    II. Series.
H61.3.D53 1983          300′.28′54          83-12326
ISBN 0-531-04676-1

# Contents

# How to Use Computers as a Resource

*This work is dedicated to Roberta, Joshua, and Sarah, who've learned more about computers than they probably wish to know*

# 1

# An Overview

In the past decade the use of the computer and in particular the micro-, or small, computer has become thoroughly ingrained in most people's lives. This has happened so quickly that most of us take for granted, or at least don't consider, the effect of computers on our daily lives. Let's follow Robert from the time he gets up in the morning until he goes to bed. As we trace his steps, see if you can count the number of times an encounter with a computer, or machines that use technology created by a computer, have taken place.

| Time | Event |
|------|-------|
| 7:00 AM | The digital clock radio goes off. Time to get ready for school. |
| 7:30 AM | Breakfast. Today's menu includes toast, hot chocolate, and bacon, all cooked in the microwave oven. |
| 7:45 AM | Start the car and drive to school. |
| 8:30 AM | A schedule change. The schedule received in homeroom doesn't allow for a lunch period. |
| 8:45 AM | First period. It's always the longest of the day. This is the time when attendance is taken. |

| 9:30 AM | Homeroom. Since this is the end of the second quarter, today is the day report cards are issued. |
| | Classes |
| 3:30 PM | School's out. Just enough time to play some arcade games before reporting for work. |
| 7:00 PM | Work's over. Time to punch out and get paid. |
| 9:00 PM | Dinner eaten and homework completed. It's time to watch TV for a while. |
| 10:00 PM | Almost time for bed. Some music would be nice before dozing off. |

Could you count the number of instances computer technology affected Robert's lifestyle? Were you aware that:

computer technology is found in clock radios?

microwave ovens contain powerful memory units that allow them to store cooking instructions?

the amount of gasoline sent to the engine of your parents' car is determined by a tiny microprocessor under the car's hood?

most school schedules and reports are printed and stored by computers?

video games are a direct outgrowth of the development of microcomputers?

much of the music on records and radio and many of the television shows we enjoy also rely on computers to produce their sounds and pictures? (Many musicians, as well as others in our society, need a basic knowledge of computers to operate their equipment properly.)

Large computers; small computers, called minicomputers; and very small computers, known as microcomputers, that can sit on desk tops, are all designed for one basic purpose—to process information according to the instructions they are given. They can be used for an infinite number of tasks: making simple calculations, playing games, teaching mathematics, or compiling budgets. But computers are only as capable or "intelligent" as the user who issues the instructions. When the user lists the instructions, the computer automatically executes them within milli-, or thousandths of, seconds.

You do not have to be a computer engineer to use a computer. The more information you have about computers, however, the better able you will be to use them to solve problems. This book is designed with that purpose in mind, especially with respect to government or civics, history, geography, economics, sociology, and anthropology—the subject areas that make up the social studies or social sciences. It will tell you a little bit about the history of computers, how they work, and how they have affected research and problem solving in social studies. It will also suggest ways in which computers might help you in your social studies classes. By seeing how social scientists use computers to solve problems, you may be able to use some of the same techniques, or methods, in solving similar types of problems.

## COMPUTER APPLICATIONS
## IN THE SOCIAL SCIENCES

As society has grown increasingly complex, governments, businesses, and educational institutions have turned to the men and women who work in the social sciences to help solve problems. The computer has become a vital tool for these social scientists. By using a computer, an urban planner can predict the direction in which a city's population is growing in order to plan new

highways. An economist for a large manufacturer can use a computer to determine economic trends over a period of time to help a company decide whether it should produce a new product. With the help of a computer one can quickly study information and test or simulate ideas to see if they might work without actually involving people. Providing quick access to published research is another way in which the computer serves as a powerful tool for the social scientist. Using this type of technology allows social scientists to spend more of their time analyzing information and less time simply collecting it

Computers are also used to store vast amounts of factual information that is needed by social scientists. For example, many libraries are now replacing their old card catalogs with computerized catalogs. To obtain a list of the library's holdings on a given subject, a user punches in one or two key words on a computer terminal and presses an "enter" key. This allows the computer to search its memory banks for all the books and articles that have these words or phrases in their titles—all in a matter of microseconds. This system gives the requested information far more quickly and in a more efficient manner than a physical search of the library stacks.

The government, one of the largest collectors of information and statistics, has long recognized the need to use technology. Since 1890 the United States Department of Commerce has used computing machines to aid the census bureau. Over the years the task of gathering the census data has become so large and cumbersome that if it were not for machines, and now large, electronic computers, we probably would not be able to gather the

*Microcomputers such as these have revolutionized the processing of information.*

[5]

data and get the valuable information we can acquire from the census. By using computers, however, we can easily find answers to our questions about the population of the United States. If we wish to find out how many men, women, and children there are in the state of Nebraska, for example, a computer will digest the question and provide the answer. Should we want more detailed information, such as how many men and women there are between ages fourteen and eighteen, the computer can break down the information to answer this request as well.

As we have seen, social scientists use computers to gather various types of information, to store that information for later use, or retrieval, and to manipulate, or handle, the information to help them solve problems. These tasks are part of what all of us do when we try to solve various problems.

As you relax at home this evening, think about the future and how you'll be able to turn on your TV to read your newspaper, take a class, or even vote, all through the aid of different types of computers. Whatever advantages and disadvantages this technology provides, social scientists will be there looking at its effects on society. They will record the history of computers, look at their geographic distribution, compare economic efficiency before and after computerization, and assess the cultural influences of computer technology.

# 2

# The Vocabulary of Computer Technology

People who use computers need to know many words that are special to their field. It's very important to understand these words so that you will understand the machines and processes that will be described throughout the rest of this book. Please take the time to look these words over and become familiar with the vocabulary of computers. Later, you can refer to this glossary as often as you need to.

*Abacus*: Ancient device (counting frame) used to do simple mathematics.

*Address*: A location in a computer's memory; provides the location of data to be processed.

*Algorithm*: A set of rules, in a definite order, that tell how to solve a problem.

*Alphanumeric*: Information that consists of both letters and numbers.

*Analog computer*: Used to deal with physical phenomena.

*ASCII*: American Standard Code for Information Interchange. Method of coding data that is used to store textual data.

*Assembler language*: Symbolic programming language that uses symbols and abbreviations to represent the function to be performed by the microprocessor.

*BASIC*: *B*eginners' *A*ll-Purpose *S*ymbolic *I*nstruction *C*ode. A high-level computer programming language.

*Bit*: Unit of information that signals the computer what it is to do. Bits are single digits in binary math. They can be either 1 or 0.

*Break*: To suspend execution of a program.

*Bug*: A program defect in either the computer hardware (machinery) or software (program).

*Byte*: A unit of information composed of eight bits. The computer treats this as a single unit.

*Cathode ray tube (CRT)*: A unit for displaying information, similar to a TV tube.

*Central processing unit (CPU)*: The section of the computer that interprets data and executes instructions.

*Chip*: A rectangular or square silicon chip on which integrated circuits are imprinted.

*COBOL*: *C*ommon *B*usiness *O*riginated *L*anguage. Computer language developed for business applications.

*Compiler*: An automatic computer coding system capable of generating and assembling a program from instructions written by a programmer or prepared by equipment manufacturers or software companies.

*Cursor*: Position indicator employed in a display on a video terminal to indicate a character to be corrected or a position in which data is to be entered.

*Data*: Information that is passed to or output from a program. There are four types of data: integer numbers, single-precision numbers, double-precision numbers, and character-string sequences (strings).

*Debug*: To correct a faulty program or operation.

*Digital computer*: A machine that uses discrete data; for example, numbers, names, and figures.

*Disk*: A device resembling a small 45-RPM record on which data is stored. Sometimes called floppy disk.

*Disk drive*: A device consisting of a spindle on which a disk or diskette can be mounted for electronically storing data.

*Flow chart*: The way in which a computer program is diagramed. It includes instructions as well as data.

*FORTRAN*: *For*mula *Tran*slation. A high-level computer language designed for scientists, mathematicians, and engineers.

*Hardware*: Computer machinery.

*Input*: To transfer data from outside the computer (from a cassette file, keyboard, etc.) into the computer's memory.

*Input device*: Used to get information and data into the system. Usually it is done with a keyboard, a cassette recorder, or a disk-drive mechanism.

*Integrated circuit*: An interconnected array of conventional electronic components fabricated on and in a single crystal of semiconductor material by etching, doping, diffusion, etc., and capable of performing a complete circuit function.

*Kilobyte, or K*: 1,024 bytes of memory. A 64K system includes 64 X 1,024 = 65,536 bytes of memory.

*Loop*: A self-contained series of instructions whose last command repeats the entire cycle.

*Memory*: The amount of data and instructions a computer can store. Usually represented in thousands of bytes by the symbol K (8K, 16K, 32K, for example).

*Memory unit*: A place in the computer where words and numbers are stored and later retrieved.

*Microcomputer*: A digital computer whose processing unit is a microprocessor.

*Microprocessor*: The electronic components of an entire central processor unit created on a single, very small silicon chip.

*Output device*: The apparatus that receives the input and puts it into a usable form for the user. Examples are a printer and a television receiver (*see Cathode ray tube*).

*Pascal*: High-level computer language. Developed for use on microcomputers with extended memory capability.

*Program*: A set of instructions to the computer that direct it to solve a problem.

*Random-access memory (RAM)*: A computer storage device which can be read from and written into. It is a changeable computer operation.

*Read-only memory (ROM)*: A computer storage device that cannot be changed in computer operation. It can only be read from.

*Software*: The computer program, and offline materials used with computer operations.

*Statement*: A line of a computer program.

*Syntax*: The "grammatical" requirements needed to be used in preparing for a command or statement. Syntax generally refers to punctuation and order of elements.

*Terminal*: A hardware device that allows the user to interact with the computer. It usually consists of a CRT device, a keyboard, and an input device such as a disk or cassette recorder.

*Time-sharing*: A system in which one or more terminals are tied together and share time allotments from a large central computer.

# 3

# From Abacus to Microcomputer

The word "computer" is derived from the Latin word for "count." Historically, the first persons who counted their fingers, toes, or the number of animals that they owned were computing. It wasn't too long before counting and keeping records of things that had been counted became complicated. Once people used up all their fingers and toes, they began to use objects to represent numbers.

Piles of rocks, tree branches, and even marks on cave walls were used to represent items that were being counted. Soon this also became a problem as trading between different communities increased. What people now needed was something that was portable, small, and able to store, or retain, information, and that allowed the user to manipulate numbers. Eventually, such a device, called the abacus, was invented to meet that need.

It may have been either the Chinese, Egyptians, or Phoenicians—or all three—who invented the abacus. No one knows for certain, as remnants of these first mechanical computational aids have been uncovered at archaeological sites of each of these ancient civilizations. The abacus was imitated and copied by virtually all of the merchant and trading civilizations throughout the world. The major functions of the abacus, manipulating numbers and storing information, are at the heart of all modern machine-oriented computational operations.

It wasn't until the seventeenth, eighteenth, and nineteenth centuries that inventors began to toy with the idea of taking the basic functions of the abacus and mechanizing, or tying machines, to them. They did this because governments and commercial ventures were unable to handle the increasingly large quantities of calculations required of them. Blaise Pascal, a French mathematician, invented such a machine in 1642 that was capable of adding and subtracting through the use of gears and moving parts. Gottfried Wilhelm Leibniz, a German mathematician (1646–1716), enhanced Pascal's calculator by adding a step-wheel that allowed its user to multiply and divide. Joseph-Marie Jacquard, at the 1801 Paris Exposition, exhibited an automated loom (for weaving) similar to ones used today, whose patterns were controlled by holes punched into cards. This was the forerunner of today's computer punch cards.

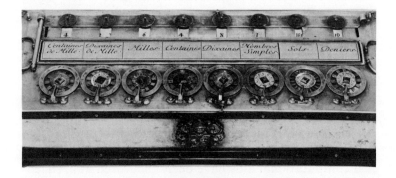

*Blaise Pascal's calculator,*
*a forerunner of today's computers*

All of these machines laid the groundwork for the English mathematician and technician Charles Babbage's "difference engine." Babbage first thought of this machine in 1812, and worked on it for over twenty years. A steam-driven device, it was supposed to compute complex mathematical tables, such as logarithms, automatically. But Babbage had financial troubles and never completed his invention. Several years later, a Swede named George Scheutz used Babbage's plans to build a machine that could carry calculations to fourteen decimal places and print the results. This machine won a gold medal at the 1855 Paris Exposition.

Many governmental agencies noted the development of these machines and discovered that they could use them to help ease their jobs. In the mid–1880s the U.S. Census Bureau held a competition to select an efficient method of tabulating the 1890 census. Reacting to this, Herman Hollerith, an American statistician, invented an electromechanical machine that could process numbers that had been fed into it by the use of punch cards.

The "first generation" of modern computers, created by men such as Howard Aiken of Harvard University and Allan Turing, an Englishman, began in the late 1930s. The automatic controlled calculator, a device that consisted of seventy-eight adding machines, and the general-purpose computer were two of the devices introduced during this era. In 1946 the first electronic computer, called ENIAC (*E*lectronic *N*umerical *I*ntegrator *a*nd *C*alculator) was unveiled. Using miles of wire, large, bulky vacuum tubes, and a cathode implant, this machine was the forerunner of modern data-processing equipment.

A major technological breakthrough occurred in 1947 when three American scientists, William Schockley, Walter Brattain, and John Bardeen, invented the transistor at Bell Laboratories. About 2 inches (5 cm)

long, the transistor was 1/200 of the size of the vacuum tube and used less than 1/100 of the power. The transistor was quickly adapted for use in radios and computers. This initiated the "second generation" of modern computers, which were less costly, smaller, and more efficient than the first.

The "third (and present) generation" of computers has been made possible through the development of the integrated circuit, the printed circuit board, and the large-scale integration (LSI) chip. This all began in 1965 when the integrated circuit made its first appearance. Over a thousand such circuits can be placed on a single silicon chip less than 1/4 inch (0.6 cm) square. The use of the chips and circuits has increased the power of computers while decreasing their price.

It was not until 1975 that the first "true" microcomputer, or small computer, was produced. These computers, although much smaller than their predecessors, were, and are, capable of doing the same types of computer operations. The "heart" of any computer, the central processing unit (CPU), which controls the computer and stores all its information, is today smaller than a dime. Along with the decreased size of computers, the use of new materials and production techniques have also aided in lowering costs. Microcomputers include all arcade games and home video machines, as well as the Atari, PET, Apple, TRS-80, Vic-20, and Sinclair ZX. Many of these can now be purchased for under two hundred dollars.

*ENIAC, the
first electronic
computer, was
developed in 1946.*

# A BRIEF SURVEY OF
# COMPUTER HISTORY

| Date | Event |
|------|-------|
| 3000 B.C. | Abacus first mechanical aid to computation. |
| A.D. 1630 | Slide rule invented by Oughtred. |
| 1664 | First mechanical calculating machine—Blaise Pascal. |
| 1671 | Machine does basic mathematic operations—Gottfried Wilhelm Leibniz. |
| 1804 | Punch cards used as machine input/output mechanisms—Joseph-Marie Jacquard. |
| 1834 | Difference and analytical engine machines. Includes basic format for modern computer—Charles Babbage. |
| 1850 | Patent issued on keypunch machine—D. D. Parmallee. |
| 1885 | First machine using punch-card concept for processing numerical data—Herman Hollerith. |
| 1890 | U.S. Bureau of Census uses Hollerith's machine to assist census count. |
| 1937 | General-purpose computer developed—Allan Turing. |
| 1944 | Mark I, first electromechanical computer. |
| 1946 | ENIAC, first electronic computer. |
| 1947 | Transistor developed at Bell Labs—John Bardeen, Walter Brattain, and William Schockley. |
| 1949 | ENIAC does five thousand additions per second. |
| 1951 | UNIVAC (*Uni*versal *A*utomatic *C*omputer), first commercially developed computer, put in use. |

| | |
|---|---|
| 1959 | Computers using transistors put in operation; PLATO, Computer Assisted Instruction Project for undergraduates, started at University of Illinois. |
| 1963 | Dartmouth University builds BASIC (*Beginning All-Purpose Symbolic Instruction Code*) time-sharing language system. |
| 1965 | "Third generation" of computers, using integrated circuits, put in operation. Public Schools in Philadelphia, New York City, and Waterford, Michigan, adopt Computer Assisted Instruction. |
| 1967 | Six percent of college students use computers. |
| 1968 | Boy Scouts of America introduce computer merit badge. |
| 1969 | U.S. Office of Education spends $35.6 million on educational computing. |
| 1970 | Introduction of large-scale integration (LSI), process of making microchips. |
| 1973 | Students at George Washington High School, in Denver, develop car-pooling program, which is disseminated nationally by Department of Transportation. |
| 1977 | Congressional hearings held on computers and the Learning Society. TRS-80, PET, and Apple microcomputer systems introduced. |
| 1979 | Northwest Regional Education Laboratory, in Portland, Oregon, establishes MICROSIFT, national clearinghouse for educational programs that run on microcomputers. |
| 1980 | Large purchases of microcomputer systems made by public schools. |
| 1981 | Intelligent video-disk computer systems used in schools. |
| 1982 | Microcomputer available for under a hundred dollars. |

# 4

# How Does
# It Work?

I t's important to understand the basics of how a computer works even if you plan only to use it and not program, or develop materials for computer use. Almost every job now has some form of computer technology associated with it, from car-assembly plants, which are controlled by computerized robots, to offices, which use computer word processors for typing and revising correspondence and other documents. Computer technology is clearly becoming an important part of our lives and our work.

In simplest language, a contemporary computer is a fast electronic calculating machine, which accepts "*input*" information in the form of digits, or numbers, processes it according to a "program" stored in its "memory," and produces the resulting "output" information.

The word "computer" encompasses a large variety of machines, widely differing in size, speed, and cost. For example, when you purchase an airline ticket, the reservation agent will input your name and flight number into a computer terminal. This terminal is connected, by telephone lines, to a large computer many miles away that has been programmed to process the information. It stores your flight number and sends the reservation agent a message indicating that there is space on the flight for you. This computer is very large both physically and in terms of the amount of memory, or storage space, it has available. Smaller machines are usually called minicomputers or microcomputers, which is a reflection of their relatively low cost, size, and computing power. The term "microcomputer" was coined in the 1970s to describe a very small computer consisting of only a few large-scale integrated-circuit packages. These computers range from desk-top size to those that are hand-held.

Although the size of a computer determines its processing power and cost and the complexity and sophistication of its design, the basic engineering concepts are essentially the same for all classes of computers. All computers have the same main parts: a central processing unit *(CPU)*, an input/output device (I/O), and a program. With the help of the chart on page 20, let's consider what each of these parts does and how they all work together in the computer.

## MEMORY

The sole function of the *memory unit* is to store programs and data. There are two types of memory devices, called the primary and the secondary storage components. Because primary storage, or main memory, is essential to computer operation, let's look at it in more detail. Primary storage is a fast memory, capable of operating in microseconds. The main memory contains a large number of storage cells that hold information, each capable or storing one *bit*, or piece of information. These cells are seldom handled individually. Instead, it is usual to deal with them in groups of fixed size. Such a group is called a *byte*, or a word. The main memory is organized so that the contents of one word can be stored or retrieved in one basic operation. To provide easy access

## COMPUTER OPERATIONS OVERVIEW

STORAGE

```
              ┌──────────────┐
              │    TAPE      │
              │     or       │
              │   DISKETTE   │
              └──────────────┘
                     ↕
INPUT                              OUTPUT
┌──────────┐  ┌──────────────┐  ┌──────────────┐
│          │  │   CENTRAL    │  │    VIDEO     │
│          │  │  PROCESSING  │  │    SCREEN    │
│ KEYBOARD │→ │     UNIT     │→ │     or       │
│          │  │              │  │   PRINTER    │
│          │  │              │  │     or       │
└──────────┘  └──────────────┘  │    both      │
                     ↕          └──────────────┘
              ┌──────────────┐
              │     ROM      │
              │     or       │
              │     RAM      │
              └──────────────┘
                  MEMORY
```

to any word in the main memory, each word location is identified with a distinct number, called an *address*.

The number of bits in each word, or byte, is often referred to as the word length of the given computer. Larger microcomputers usually have thirty-two or more bits in a byte; smaller ones have between twelve and twenty-four, while some have only four or eight bits per byte. This is what characterizes the size of a computer.

Data is usually manipulated within the machine in units. It is essential to be able to find any word location, or address, within the main memory as quickly as possible. A memory where any location can be reached by specifying its address is called a *random-access memory (RAM)*. A section of memory reserved for system use only is a *read-only memory (ROM)*.

For example, a computer that had 8K, or eight thousand bits of memory, would be able to process, manipulate, and store eight thousand individual letters or numbers. It would divide the eight thousand into ROM and RAM memory. If the computer needed two thousand bits of memory to operate, to turn on and so forth, this would be the ROM memory. Six thousand bits would then be left in the RAM memory to execute or produce various programs.

## CENTRAL PROCESSING UNIT (CPU)

The devices that control the computer and the arithmetic and logic circuits, or controlling mechanisms, are usually referred to as the *central processing unit (CPU)*.

Execution of most operations within the computer takes place in the arithmetic and logic unit (ALU). Consider a typical example. Suppose two numbers located in the main memory are to be added. They are brought into the arithmetic unit where the actual addition is carried out. The sum may then be stored in the memory.

[21]

## INPUT AND OUTPUT (I/O)

The computer in your classroom probably has a type-writer-style keyboard and either a viewing screen or TV set connected to the computer. With this equipment, you can put information into the computer (input) and receive results (output) after it has been processed. Other standard input/output (I/O) equipment includes tape recorders and *disk drives*.

Despite the fact that the same equipment may sometimes be used for both input and output of information (for example, a tape recorder), these two functions are different. The input unit accepts coded information from the outside world. The information is either stored in the memory for later reference or immediately handled by the arithmetic and logic circuitry, which performs the desired operations. The processing steps are determined by a "program" stored in the memory. Finally, the results are sent back to the outside world through the output unit. All these actions are coordinated by the control unit, the CPU.

Examples of ways of inputting information are punched cards, magnetic disks, and magnetic tape. These are often used in machines with large memory. A familiar input device is the typewriter-style keyboard which is often attached to the console of a computer, sometimes with a video screen attached.

Examples of output devices are card punches, magnetic tape drives, and disk drives. An output device that prints data in an easily read form is the "line printer," which prints an entire line at once. The I/O also allows the operator to store information—that is, to save it to use at a later date. This is done on tape or disk.

Taken together the memory, input/output units and the CPU provide the computer with the necessary tools for storing and processing information. Their operations must be coordinated in some organized way, and this is the task of the control unit, the CPU. It is the "nerve center" of the whole machine, which is used to send control signals to all other units. Much of the control center circuitry is physically distributed throughout the machine and connected by a large set of control lines (wires), which carry the signals used for timing and synchronization of events in all units.

## THE PROGRAM

The information fed into computers is of two types: instructions and data. Instructions are explicit commands which:

- govern the transfer of information within the machine, as well as between the machine and I/O devices, and
- specify the arithmetic and logic operations to be performed.

A set of instructions which perform a task is called a "program." For example:

```
110 PRINT "ROSES ARE RED"
120 PRINT "VIOLETS ARE BLUE"
```

is a program. It tells the computer to print "Roses are red, violets are blue" as the first two lines of the output.

Usually a completed program is stored in the memory of the computer. When the program runs, the CPU fetches the instructions comprising the program from the memory and performs the desired operations. Instructions are normally executed in the order in which they are stored, although it is possible to vary the order. The behavior of the computer is under the complete control of the stored program unless told differently by the computer operator.

Different computers use different types of languages in their program. The computer language is a combination of numbers, letters, and direct commands telling the computer what to do. Most microcomputers use a language called *BASIC* (*B*eginners' *A*ll-Purpose *S*ymbolic *I*nstruction *C*ode) as their language. The programs used on these machines are written in the BASIC language.

## SUMMARY

Look again at the chart on page 20. Can you trace the following steps in the operation of a typical general-purpose computer?

1. It accepts information (program and data) through the input unit and transfers it to the memory through the CPU.
2. Information stored in the memory is carried, under program control, into the ALU to be processed.
3. All activities inside the machine are under the control of the CPU.

The typical microcomputer in a classroom will consist of:

1. an input device in the form of a typewriter-style keyboard
2. a video display unit (TV set on screen)
3. a memory unit (imbedded within the *hardware*)
4. an input/output device that also allows for storage

This man is using a microcomputer whose input/
output devices are a keyboard and a disk drive,
located beneath the viewing screen to his right.
Programs for the computer are stored on the floppy
disk that he holds in his hand and which will be
inserted in the disk drive mechanism to activate
the computer. A "line printer," sitting beside the
viewing screen, completes the microcomputer system.

A few additional words about the storage requirement discussed earlier may be useful at this point. Two devices are used for storage purposes with microcomputers.

1. *Magnetic cassette tape* is used with a specially adapted audio cassette player/recorder. The cassette tape is read sequentially. Thus, to find a program named JOIN, the computer has to read from the beginning of the casette tape or wherever it is arbitrarily started, through all the programs on the cassette until it finds JOIN. This process can be time-consuming.

2. *Disk storage* (floppy disk) is much faster than cassette tape. This is because material contained on the disk can be accessed randomly. To find the JOIN program stored on a disk, the computer simply finds the program's disk location in a directory at a "know" location on the disk, then goes directly to that particular location. Since disks take up less room than tape storage, a larger amount of data and programs can be stored in a smaller space. However, disk storage is more expensive than tape storage.

# 5

# Solving Problems
# with Computers

After you've begun to understand how a computer works, you might start to think about the ways in which computers deal with various types of problems. Computers are used in a variety of ways and settings. As with other types of problem-solving activities, computer problems, or programs, use a series of logical steps. The procedure in which we define, understand, and solve a computer problem is called an *algorithm*, and it is similar to some social studies activities.

In this problem-solving process, first a problem is recognized. For instance, let's say you decided to turn on your TV set to watch one of your favorite shows. You go to the set, twist the on-off knob, and nothing happens. Immediately you realize that there is a problem—the set won't work. Having recognized the problem, you begin to wonder why the TV is not working. This is called formulating a hypothesis about the problem. After deciding what might be wrong, you test your hypothesis to see if you are correct. For example, the set might not be plugged into the wall outlet, or the aerial could be broken, or a tube could be worn out. You would probably test one at a time, until you had solved the problem.

As you can see, a solution to a problem is generated from hypotheses, or suppositions. Also, inferences, or conclusions, about other problems of a similar nature can be developed. Suppose, in this case your set was unplugged. A reasonable inference for you to draw would be to always make sure your TV set is plugged in before turning it on.

The algorithm process of solving a computer problem is quite similar. Carin E. Horn and James L. Poirot in their book *Computer Literacy* (1981) list five steps in the computer problem-solving process:

1. The computer problem must be fully understood.
2. The desired results must be fully understood.
3. The strategy for problem-solving must be logical.
4. The algorithm, or problem, must be coded into a computer language.
5. The computer must be run to solve the problem.

Programmers—people who solve problems with computers—usually use a flow chart to represent the problem-solving process. The symbols on a flow chart indicate ways in which to solve a particular problem. Flow charts help the programmer to see the basic organization of the problem and to understand how to solve it with the computer. The chart on page 29 shows the symbols that someone preparing a flow chart might use.

Flow chart symbols are available on plastic templates like the one shown in the diagram on page 30. These templates have become part of the "tools of the trade" for all computer programmers. These might also be used by engineers, builders, or scientists.

A programmer looking at the algorithm shown on page 31, would recognize that this is a chart that diagrams the solution to a typical computer problem.

For example, let's say you want to add the series of numbers 10, 20, and 30. You would input the three numbers, ask the computer to add, or process, them, and get

## BASIC FLOW CHART SYMBOLS

1. Marks the beginning or end of a flow chart. A single word such as START, BEGIN, STOP, or END is sufficient to define this operation.

2. The input/output symbol, which indicates that information is to be obtained from an outside source (inputed) or to be given to an outside source (outputed).

3. Used to indicate an operation process or to define a variable element in the program.

4. Used whenever a decision is to be made.

Additional symbols for specifying a particular medium of input or output or another operation are sometimes used.

Used for punched cards.

Used to allow flow lines to connect.

Used when a "hands-on" paper copy is required.

FLOW CHART TEMPLATE

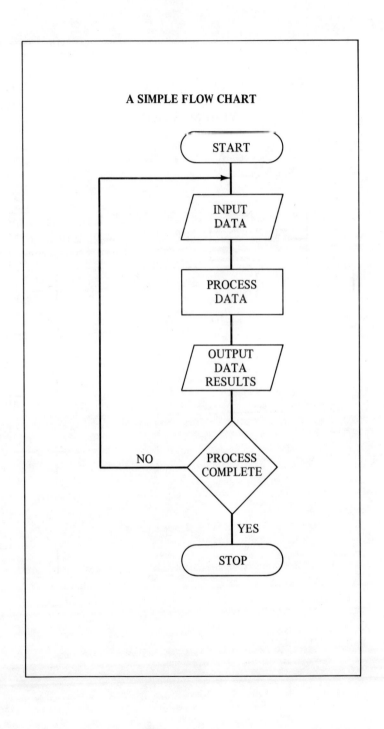

A SIMPLE FLOW CHART

START

INPUT
DATA

PROCESS
DATA

OUTPUT
DATA
RESULTS

NO — PROCESS
COMPLETE

YES

STOP

# VETOING A BILL

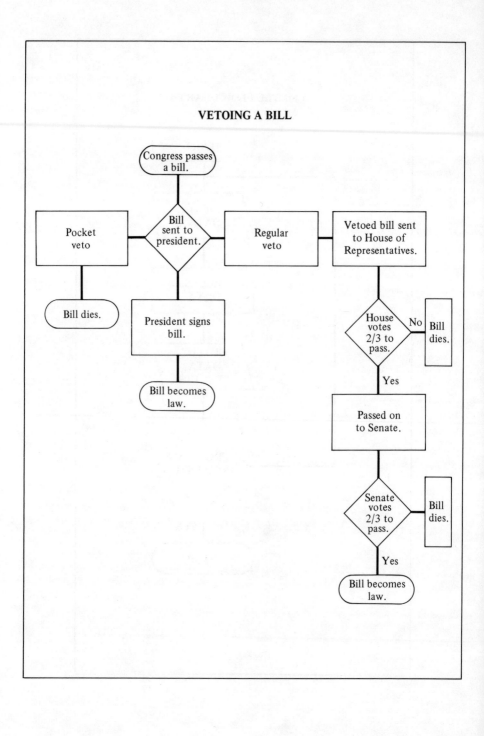

# CAN YOU BE PRESIDENT OF THE UNITED STATES?

Want To Be President

Only 15 years old; cannot be president

No

At least 35 years old

Yes

Born in Canada; cannot be president

No

Natural-born citizen

Yes

Lived in U.S. only 4 years; cannot be president

No

Lived in U.S. past 14 years

Yes

Meet qualifications; can run for president

the output, or 60. If that was all you wanted, the process would be complete. However, if you wanted to add more numbers, or subtract some numbers, you would have to go back to the input and begin again.

The flow chart shown on page 32 might be developed to show what happens if a bill passed by the U.S. Congress is vetoed by the president. Note that it does not explain what a veto is; nor does it identify a pocket veto. It merely pictures the steps in the veto procedure, or veto problem-solving process.

After looking at this example, could you design a flow chart to solve a social studies problem? For example, suppose you had to flow-chart the requirements for being president of the United States. First you would have to know that you must be at least thirty-five years of age, a resident of the United States for the past fourteen years, and a natural-born citizen: The flow chart might look like the one shown on page 33.

See if you can make a flow chart for the following problems:

1. How is a treaty ratified in the United States Senate?

2. What are the requirements for running for the U.S. House of Representatives?

3. What are the major rivers of the United States?

Now that you are familiar with computers, the way they solve problems, and how to write problem-solving or algorithm solutions to them, we will look at how social scientists use computers to aid them in their work.

# 6

# Computers and the Social Sciences:

## HISTORY, ANTHROPOLOGY, AND POLITICAL SCIENCE

The way people use computers depends upon their particular needs. The computer, in this light, becomes a technological tool we use to find solutions to problems. Just as the effectiveness of a dictionary, map, or encyclopedia depends on your skill in using it, so the effectiveness of a computer depends on your ability to locate the necessary information stored in it and to interpret the data it gives you. In this chapter and the next, we shall examine some of the ways computers are used by social scientists—both as aids in solving problems and as tools in research. This chapter will review computer applications that can be used in history, anthropology, and political science. The following chapter will look at how computers are used in geography, economics, sociology, and ecology.

## HISTORY

History is the record of the past. While some people may think of these records literally as birth dates, places where battles took place, or winners in a certain election, history is more than these. It encompasses the stories of all civilizations from ancient times to the recent past. The historians' job is to trace the factual information of a particular civilization or society—dates, places, people, and events—and to interpret the effect of these elements on their own society. Historians also consider what effect past generations have had on those who came after them. In doing this type of research all types of data and resources may have to be examined and studied.

To understand political life in the United States at the turn of the twentieth century, a historian might focus on prominent men or women of the time such as business leaders, artists, or athletes. Noting the jobs or daily activities of these individuals, as well as the games they played and the books they read, helps in interpreting how they lived and why they reacted as they did to particular societal issues. For instance, in examining the status of children in the nineteenth century, and how prominent people felt about them, a historian might want to read laws concerning child labor to determine the working conditions that children experienced. This might also reveal how children of that period spent their leisure time.

How could a computer aid in this process? First, and foremost, it could store and retrieve various bits of data the historian gathered while researching a particular project. The child labor laws, for example, could be located, copied onto a computer diskette or tape, and stored for later use as needed. In this effort the historian would use both a large computer to gather the information and a microcomputer to use the information as needed in the research project. This process, known as information retrieval, is being implemented at various museums, government agencies, and other places where historical records and archives are currently housed. Not only does this process make the task of the historian easier by centrally locating important records, but it functions as a means of preserving records. That is, records

[36]

on paper or other perishable materials are transferred to computer records, where they will be preserved for an extended period of time.

The other processes that the historian uses, analysis and interpretation, also benefit from computerization. As with piecing together a puzzle, the historian sometimes looks at different parts before putting the whole "puzzle" together. The historian who is interested in the games that children played in the early nineteenth century might be able to find out not only the kind of play that children engaged in but the kind of equipment that they used. This in turn could reflect on the kinds of sporting goods or toy businesses that were profitable during this time. The computer allows the historian to take apart various pieces of a puzzle and manipulate them. This is called data transformation or data analysis. Questions such as why certain things happen as they do, or whether the order in which things occur plays a role in their relationship, can be answered by using these analyses.

As you become more familiar with the computer and develop some programming skills, you will be able to solve several kinds of historical problems with the use of the computer. For example, you might begin to investigate your family lineage, using the computer to store the information as it became available and then retrieve it in the order desired. Graphics could enhance this program until eventually a design like the one on page 38 might be developed.

You might also solve that problem by purchasing a ready-made program. There are several commercial genealogy programs available for use with a variety of microcomputers:

1. *Apple Tree.* For the APPLE II, by J. Fiske Software Systems, Inc., One University Place, New York, NY 10003.

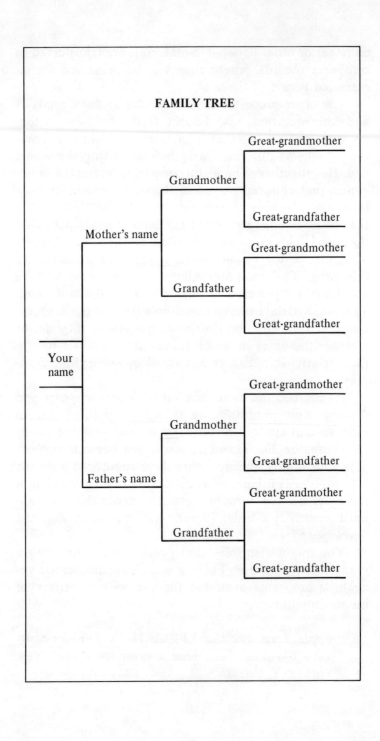

**FAMILY TREE**

Great-grandmother

Grandmother

Great-grandfather

Mother's name

Great-grandmother

Grandfather

Great-grandfather

Your name

Great-grandmother

Grandmother

Great-grandfather

Father's name

Great-grandmother

Grandfather

Great-grandfather

2. *Genealogy.* For TRS 80 Model III, by Frank Lercher, 2950 Espana Court, Fairfax, CA 22051.

3. *Genie.* For TRS 80 Model II, Apple III, and IBM Personal Computer, by Sinclair G. Cannen, 895 South 770 West, Woodcross, UT 84087.

4. *Roots/89* and *Roots/M.* For Heath Kit H-89, by Commsoft, 665 Maybell Ave., Palo Alto, CA 94306.

Note: Since each computer's ability to use a computer language is different, each computer requires a program that matches its language.

Also remember that you, as a student, must be able to locate facts, make judgments, and evaluate information. The computer simply manipulates the data as the user sees fit.

## ANTHROPOLOGY

Anthropology is the study of humans—their evolution, their behavior, their language, and their customs. The manner, or approach, in which anthropologists look at humans can take different forms. In part, anthropology resembles biological science, since it deals with humans as a living species; and behavioral science, because it looks at the actions of humans in group settings.

Probably the most familiar of all the types of anthropologists are the archaeologists—the "diggers" who comb the globe searching for ancient cities and civilizations. Most of you have seen pictures of these excavations where fossils, tools, and other artifacts of early life have been uncovered.

Closely related to archaeology is the work of physical anthropologists, who examine biological relationships between humans and other species. They compare anatomical structures and search for evidence of past forms

[39]

of life that resembled humans. Physical anthropologists look at bone structure, and changes in teeth, hair, and other physical attributes over generations. Sir Louis Leaky spent most of his life looking for the physical link between modern human beings and their prehistoric ancestors.

Some anthropologists are interested in the study of human fossils, which is a part of the science of paleontology. This study includes the reconstruction of prehistoric remains, from which the paleontologist notes the physical shape and size of past generations of humans.

Other anthropologists, called ethologists, compare the physical structures and behavior of animals to that of humans to better understand human behavior. Jane Goodall has spent years studying chimpanzees in their natural habitat so that she might draw some conclusions about both human and animal behavior patterns. Studies of this type are called ethologies.

Linguists are anthropologists who study languages. They are not merely interested in learning the language; they look for its roots and compare it with other languages to discover similarities and differences. They also look for relationships and patterns among languages.

Cultural anthropologists look at humans as they interact with each other in groups. They study patterns of behavior and lifestyles. As with other anthropologists, they look for similarities and differences in behavior patterns. A cultural anthropologist might investigate the kinds of music people like and the types of clothes they wear. They might ask if certain members of the society, such as teenagers, like different kinds of food than the older members of that society.

Computers and computer technology are currently being used in many phases of anthropological research and study. Physical anthropologists use computers to examine how humans have changed over time. They do this through the use of models. Just as you might make a model of an airplane or car, these scientists are taking the evidence that exists about the way humans looked thousands of years ago and developing models that try to reconstruct the ways they lived. Finding a piece of human remains near what is now a dry lake bed may lead to the conclusion that the diet of people who lived in that locale consisted at least partly of fish they caught in the lake. Using a computer, the anthropologist could develop a series of questions that ask what these people did with the fish once they caught them, how they may have caught the fish, and if they could have passed this knowledge on to future generations. The model might also indicate what these prehistoric humans might have done when the lake dried out.

Paleontologists use computers to find out how old a fossil may be. First they measure the amount of carbon and carbon decay in a structure. By enlarging this on a computer and comparing the data to that of other bones from the same era, they can approximate the age of the find. This is possible because all of us have carbon in our bodies and it decays at the same rate.

Linguists and cultural anthropologists use the computer to store and retrieve data. Using the audio, or sound, capabilities available on many computers, linguists are now able to reconstruct ancient dialects of languages long since unheard. This can be done by programming the computer with known pitches and ranges of speech and having the computer compare these with known sound variations of human speech. This process, done in microseconds, could take years if done without the aid of the computer.

Archaeologists have used computers to help uncover potential excavation sites. Using computerized sensors that bounce sound waves below the earth's surface, researchers can now scan an area for items of interest in order to decide whether to dig there. This has been done in many places around the world, and the method was also used, without success, by several expeditions searching the ocean floor for the legendary lost city of Atlantis. The sensors, however, have been able to find the ships the *Titanic* and the *Andrea Doria*, which were sunk many years ago.

One of the other tasks that anthropologists do is to record behavior patterns. The computer is the perfect tool for this task. For example, if a researcher wanted to find out what kinds of foods students eat or throw away during school lunches, he or she would have to keep records of these events. This might eventually become time-consuming. Recording these events on a computer as they occur would free the anthropologist to observe why these patterns of behavior develop. To the anthropologist, the key subject is the relationships that develop between people. Using the computer can free researchers from repetitive tasks and allow them to concentrate on evaluation of the information.

You might try a study in your own school lunchroom. What kinds of foods are served on each particular day of the week? How many students buy these foods? Which ones do they eat, and which ones do they throw away? Ask students why they are eating some of the food but throwing some away. The answers to these questions may also require that you find out what kinds of foods students like and dislike and what kinds are served in their homes. After you've obtained this information, you might analyze it and develop a set of statements about the kinds of foods different groups prefer.

## POLITICAL SCIENCE

Government and civics are the study of how people organize their societies and the rules they make to keep their societies running smoothly. This study is also called

*These Brazilian government employees are studying data that has been processed in a large computing center. The Brazilian government uses computers to compile its national census and to study the most economic uses of land and natural resources, as well as transportation and communication facilities.*

political science. Experts in the field are usually called political scientists.

Political scientists seek explanations of why governments began as well as looking at the decisions that they make today. Political scientists also study a wide range of topics relating to government. Many concern themselves with the processes by which members of a society seek to influence governmental decision making; this is what we call politics. Others study how governments and individuals administer the authority given to them by the society. Still others concentrate on international relations, or how one society's governmental structure is related to another's.

The political scientist uses a variety of information or resources to develop conclusions about the issues they are studying. The kind of records they use are dependent on the problem under consideration. Examples are:

1. Budgets of the U.S. government as well as those of states and localities.

2. Records of cases that have been heard in federal and state court systems.

3. Debates about the way laws have been passed.

4. Records of court cases.

5. Records of the way people have voted.

Information technology has become a powerful new tool for the political scientist. Instantaneous retrieval of voting and election results, for example, can help in establishing patterns of behavior and predict trends in elections. Since 1952, the major television networks have used computers to count votes and analyze the results in congressional and presidential elections. Many people however, have criticized the networks for using technology this way. They say that by predicting an outcome of a national political race, such as the presidency, before all

[44]

the polling places have closed, some potential voters may not vote, feeling that their candidate has already been defeated.

Although computer technology may present a dilemma for some in predicting elections, there is no doubt that political candidates now rely heavily on computers when it comes to opinion polls. Many candidates depend on polls taken for them by political scientists to develop their strategies for winning an election. For instance, a candidate might commission a poll of his or her constituents about a particular issue concerning the burning of garbage in their area. The person conducting the poll would develop a series of questions about the garbage issue such as:

1. Do you think garbage should be burned?
2. If not, what way other than burning should be used in disposing of garbage?
3. Would you like to live near a garbage dump?

This poll will not include all persons within the candidate's election area, but merely a scientific sample. After collecting the data, computers will provide a printout indicating preferences on the issue in question. The politician could then make a decision about the burning of garbage with the voters of the district in mind.

Taking a poll of your classmates' opinions on an issue that is being discussed in your school can be an excellent way to sharpen your skills in political analysis and also increase your understanding of how computers help political scientists. First decide what kind of information about your classmates you might wish to have. This would include name, age, sex, and place of residence. Just as political scientists might use this information to understand how different age groups vote, so can you. These factors are called demographic variables.

Next you must choose the questions you wish to ask.

This is an important step because the information you receive depends on the questions you ask. In preparing these questions you must also ask yourself, Why am I asking them, and what type of information do I hope to obtain? The procedure is called hypothesis development. Remember our garbage poll? What kind of information would you get about garbage from your classmates? Would it be important?

Upon obtaining the requested information you then must decide what to do with it. Will you merely record it, or will you try to see what it means if you analyze it? Political scientists deal with these same sets of issues as they gather information.

Finally, what kinds of generalizations can you infer from your study? Do the results have broad implications? Could this same study be repeated by another researcher? Would the results be the same?

This process might be used to conduct a mock election campaign poll in your school. First a poll would be developed based on the answers to a series of questions about the candidate, issues concerning the voters, and demographic factors. These questions would try to determine whom students would vote for, why they would vote for a particular candidate, and which age groups might vote for which candidate. Next, the poll would be administered among a part of the general population of your school, and the results would be tabulated, stored, and recorded.

An analysis of voting trends could then be made by breaking down the demographic factors by voting patterns. For instance, we could find out how many fourteen-year-old freshman girl students would vote for a particular candidate versus the fourteen-year-old freshman boy students. Predictions about the outcome of the election would be made based on the results of the poll. After the election the results of the poll could be compared with the actual election returns to determine the accuracy of the predictions as well as to study student voting patterns. Analysis of these could lead to some conclusions about voting patterns, age-group voter preferences, and candidate appeal to various groups within the society.

This process, which is part of what the political scientist does, can be used in conjunction with a computer program. Instead of recording the above information on paper, it would be transferred to a computer disk. This would allow it to be stored for later use for comparison or other purposes. If your class has a computer, you might try to write a political poll program for this purpose.

# 7

## Computers and the Social Sciences:

### GEOGRAPHY, ECONOMICS, SOCIOLOGY, AND ECOLOGY

Many people picture geographers as men and women who spend most of their time drawing maps. To be sure, geography does include the study and use of maps, the field known as cartography. Geographers, however, do much more than map making. They are involved in space exploration as part of teams that are investigating life forms throughout the solar system, they help plan where new cities might be built, they are consultants to government agencies which are trying to deal with pollution and other societal problems, and they work with other social scientists in tracking social and cultural trends in our society.

However, map making is still a very important part of geographers' work, so we'll discuss it first. Today geographers use many technological advances, including computers, as part of their work to help secure knowledge about places and land forms.

Beginning with ancient Greek cartographers, or map makers, we have long sought an accurate picture of our environment. Today, thanks to the National Aeronautic and Space Administration's (NASA) Landstat satellites, we have been able to obtain an accurate pictorial view of earth from over 500 miles (805 km) in space. Circling the earth in polar orbit, each of the satellites photographs the earth in strips 115 miles (185 km) wide. These photographs are transmitted to earth relay stations by computer and made into large maps. The Landstat satellites are able to take their photographs through the use of sensing devices that reflect light.

Using Landstat photos, scientists have detected air and water pollution sites. Geologists have been able to track oil and mineral deposits. Volcanic eruptions and their aftermaths, including the ash clouds, have also been detected and traced. This tool has become important to other segments of the scientific community: agricultural experts, who are now able to identify soil and crop problems worldwide; meteorologists, who can see the effects of weather conditions; and, of course, geographers, who now have a source from which they can reproduce the earth's physical changes quickly and efficiently. This has allowed geographers to make accurate and precise maps that note these changes quickly.

Landstat is not the only satellite that has produced computer-aided maps. *Voyager 1* and *2* and the *Explorer* probes all used computer sensor devices to transmit pictures of the moon, Mars, and other distant points in our solar system back to earth. These maps have greatly expanded our knowledge of the solar system.

Computer mapping techniques allow for more than just places and names. Data about economic conditions and cultural and social influences can also be programmed into the computer. The result is a far-ranging map that includes all these factors.

For example, a company planning a new factory can feed into a computer all the variables it is looking for at a potential site, such as water, land size, size of labor force, and availability of certain raw materials. The computer can then generate a map for a specific area of the country that contains these factors.

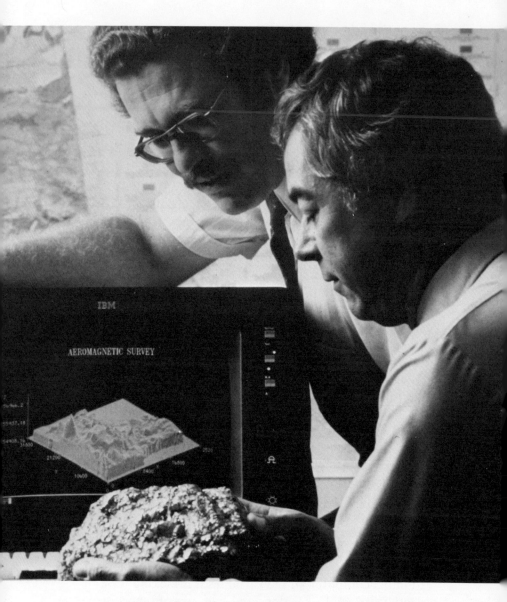

*Mining engineers use a computer model to study land formations. The information they gain will help them make decisions about future exploration.*

Computer graphics have also allowed for two-and three-dimensional maps to be made. And, computers can also create what are called dynamic maps, which show geographic changes over a period of time. For example, a geographer can see how the course of a river or the shape of a mountain has changed over the years due to climatic conditions. This can be done in a matter of moments. Changes in cultural conditions, such as population shifts or the growth and decline of cities, can also be shown. The ability of computers to store, retrieve, and portray data has helped geographers in these studies.

The fact that many of the graphic capabilities of large computers are also available in microcomputers can help students develop their own maps. Almost all microcomputers have graphic boards that can be added to the basic computer. With this attachment and some knowledge of plotting points on a computer screen, all types of maps and charts can be reproduced and stored. Even without a graphics board, once the user learns the plotting points, or where lines and colors on the screen are located, reproducing visuals becomes a relatively easy task.

As we said earlier, geographers do much more than make maps, and computers are an important part of those other activities. Geographers have used computers to examine the physical environment we live in. For example, computer technology is used to predict the changes in the earth that occur in earthquakes. Seismographs are attached to computers to indicate the size, location, and duration of earthquakes. The San Andreas fault line in California is under constant computer monitoring for possible shifts and changes. These computers act as an early-warning earthquake device.

Soil reclamation projects and river navigation are two areas that have been aided by computer technology. For the first time we can use a computer to project the effects of a change in soil conditions or erosion on a community or region. For example, a computer is attached to a scale, or reduced, model of the entire Mississippi River region, built by the Army Corps of Engineers. By providing the computer with information on rainfall, the Corps can have a model of what will happen to the soil if 18 inches (45.7 cm) of rain fall, for example, on St. Louis, Missouri, and its effects on Memphis, Tennessee. This is called simulation. Environmental, social, and economic factors can also be put into the simulation to determine what the human costs of a flood or an earthquake might be, as well as the natural costs. Also, this simulation can be used to aid in the navigation of river vessels on the Mississippi, especially when changes in the river's course occur.

## ECONOMICS

Economists study issues of scarcity, wants, needs, and choices as these concepts affect a society. Studying how a scarcity of finite resources can be used to satisfy an over-abundance of human wants takes up a great deal of the economist's time and expertise. Every society has a mechanism, called an economic system, which decides the types of goods and services that will be produced, for whom they will be produced, and in what quantity. Any economic system is based on laws, customs, culture, and political philosophy, as well as on the evolutionary process that developed it.

The arena where economic activity takes place is called the marketplace. This is where the allocation of goods and services occurs, based on supply, demand, price, and the producer's ability to satisfy the consumer's wants and needs. The marketplace can be controlled, externally, by governments or suppliers who have a vested interest in moving the market in a particular direction, or it can be left alone to fluctuate and respond to market conditions. Most exchanges (buying and selling) in the marketplace are voluntary and are facilitated through the pricing of the goods or services being exchanged or the amount of money a consumer is willing to spend on them.

There are a number of ways economists study these mechanisms. Using an institutional approach, the economist investigates the economic institutions of the society—the governmental and private agencies that direct the economic system as well as the laws and judicial decisions that affect the economic decisions of these institutions. An economist might ask, for example, What role does, or should, the government play in the allocation of resources? What happens when the government allocates or rations resources? How does government policy in one area affect the marketplace in another area? For instance, what would be the economic effect if the government rationed gasoline? How would this affect the marketplace?

Another approach to economics is to study long- and short-term economic goals. Who sets these goals? Are they attainable? What economic trade-offs will have to be used to achieve them? For instance, what kinds of decisions will have to be made if the society is to meet the goal of bringing down inflation? Will the cost of reducing inflation be increased unemployment and decreased demand for goods and services? Is this trade-off acceptable to reach this goal?

Still another area the economist studies is the economic role of individuals and groups in the society and how they affect the marketplace. The decisions of consumers, workers, and students all play a role in the marketplace. Questions such as, How do these groups make choices? Why do they make certain economic decisions rather than others? What kinds of information should be

[53]

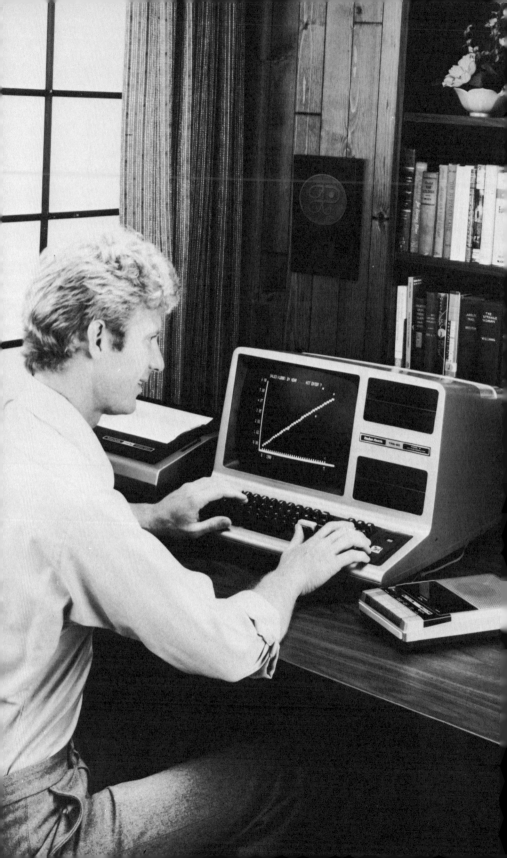

made available to them to help them make decisions? And should the government help protect these groups against problems?

Finally, many economists compare different economic systems and study how each operates. They compare efficiency, productivity, and the ability of each system to reach the goals set by its society. They note changes and carefully chart the decision-making processes in these economies. Their interpretations of other economies may directly affect the United States economy, if they are used by companies or individuals in our society who seek to provide goods and services that are lacking in other economies. At the same time, of course, economists in other countries are also looking at our economy to see what goods and services are not being provided by our system. A prime example can be noted when one looks at the kinds of stereo equipment for sale. Most is produced in Japan because of market conditions in the U.S. that make it profitable to sell Japanese goods.

Technology can assist the economist in making projections and analyses of economic conditions, particularly conditions affected by supply, demand, and cost. In other words, what goods will people buy or sell, and why? One can view, graphically, the effects of prices and use the computer to project future demands. If you start a candy business and sell candy at twenty-five cents a box, how many boxes will you sell? You won't know this until you actually sell the candy and count your sales. Once

*With the help of a
computer, an economist
studies the past sales
of a business in order
to help the owner plan
for future expansion.*

[55]

you have collected this data, you might experiment a bit by varying the price and noting how much you've sold at one price versus another price. After a few weeks you might have collected enough data to indicate the demand for candy at a certain price.

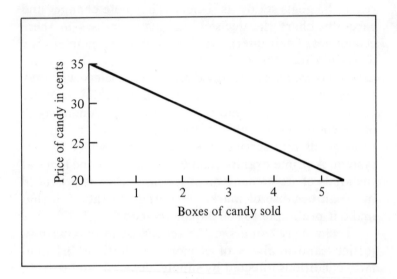

Based on this data, shown in the diagram above, we might conclude that the lower the price, the more candy would be sold. However, factors such as rent for space to store the candy and the cost of delivering it to customers might prevent you from selling candy at this price. We have used the computer to help plan our costs.

Not only can the computer help in economic planning, it can also help in personal finance. Computer programs are now available that enable the user to compute budgets and checking accounts. Called "electronic worksheets," these programs function as calculators and allow forecasting of costs and budgets through the use of sophisticated programming.

Let's say you wish to balance your c
forecast how much money you will have al.
your bills. The process is not unlike a governm
omist planning how much surplus, or deficit, the c
will have after it takes in all its tax revenues and pays
obligations. The computer display might look like this.

---

Income for this month: $1,000    Income for the year: $12,000

---

Expenditures:   $100 Car payment
                 200 Rent
                 200 Food
                 200 Utility bills
                 100 Miscellaneous
                $800 Expenditures for month
Expenditures for this year—$8,000
                        Savings for the year—$4,000

---

This type of program is called an information and
data management program. It gives the consumer, or the
person preparing a budget, a tool in the process of deciding how to use the available resources. Forecasts similar
to these that a professional economist might use could be
prepared by using a system of this type. You might prepare such a budget forecast based on how much money
you earn, should you have a job, or on your allowance, if
you get one from your parents.


## SOCIOLOGY

Sociologists are concerned with the study of human
behavior as it affects groups. They also examine ideas

that influence behavior. As with anthropologists, sociologists can be classified as behavioral scientists. For their studies sociologists use interviews, surveys, and questionnaires, as well as observation of people.

Within the broad field of sociology, individual researchers look at a variety of societal behaviors. Demographers study population growth and patterns, criminologists look at reasons for unusual, antisocial behavior patterns, urban sociologists study the way city life has changed the family and the way individuals relate to each other. Other sociologists study the ways in which income and education determine how people live. In essence, sociologists are concerned with people, their lives, and the motivations for their behavior.

Sociologists also delve into the nature of a particular culture. For example, they might analyze the food people in a particular society consume, the cars they drive, the papers they read, the media they view and listen to, and the many other ingredients that make up a culture. Their work is done by first examining items from the culture and interviewing individuals who live in that society. Then they analyze the collected information and summarize the data.

Technology has afforded sociologists previously unavailable information. Demographers can now chart the lives of entire groups of people not only in select locales but regionally, nationally, and even internationally. This helps, particularly, in analyzing why people move and live where they do. Analysis can also indicate when people are moving. As governments plan programs, they need to know where the populace is going to be located. In the United States, for instance, the population seems to be moving away from the cities of the Northeast and Midwest and into the South and West. Based on this information, demographers have built population projection models to try to guess where people might live as they move. These models, used in both the public and

*At the Red Cross headquarters in Geneva, Switzerland, this woman uses a computer to trace political refugees in an effort to reunite families that have been scattered over the world.*

private sectors, help government and businesses to make decisions about where projects and plants will be located.

Criminologists use technology to study crime statistics and patterns. The United States Department of Justice maintains a national computer network to which local and state police agencies are attached. Thus, this system ties together federal, state, and local law enforcement agencies and helps all these groups search for wanted criminals. The social scientist, however, can also use the materials generated by this system to spot criminal trends and locations. This may be useful in planning where to beef up police forces and in finding out where crimes have happened and are likely to happen.

The urban sociologist can use computer technology to collect and store information about people in cities. Later they can compare the data, study and analyze it. Answers to questionnaires and other types of research data can be processed quickly with this technology as these scientists seek information about people who live in large metropolitan areas.

As television and other communication systems become linked to computers, studies can be started to look at behavioral changes caused by exposure to mass media. Television programs, movies, or segments of each, might be played and people's responses recovered immediately by a microcomputer. Specific places in these media could be marked as stopping points where questions would be asked of the viewer via the computer. The viewer's answers would be available immediately, and the computer would mark the place on the tapes. These studies might lead to changes in advertising patterns or the types of television programs that are produced.

The way people react to certain items could be recorded and monitored with the use of the computer to chart group-versus-individual behavior patterns. Segments of this process are already being done in hospitals

[60]

and mental institutions in terms of a patient's progress. A set of behaviors is prescribed, checked on a daily basis, and later analyzed as to effectiveness.

The sociologist will play a large role in determining the overall effects of the introduction of computers as they begin to become available to large segments of the society. Changes in behavior in schools, business, and government will be monitored and analyzed. Also, and perhaps far more important, will be the way in which the information or data generated by these machines is used.

## ECOLOGY AND
## ENVIRONMENTAL STUDIES

Social scientists concerned with ecological and environmental problems help bridge the gap between social and scientific issues. Ecologists may focus on studies of population and the role humans take in the environment, or they may look at natural resources and the contributions they make to the growth of a society. Still others may investigate the changing roles of human and natural resources as they relate to technology. Topics that these scientists may evaluate include energy, pollution, conservation, and use of wildlife resources.

Computer technology assists in these studies by allowing the social scientist an environmental planning device. Problems that might be touched upon include deciding how much gas, oil, or coal we will need; resolving environmental issues and setting standards; determining whether and where atomic power plants will be built; and deciding who should pay for the cleanup of the air.

This can be done in a variety of ways but is most often done in a simulation exercise. Suppose an environmentalist is assigned the task of determining how to allocate limited natural resources in the wake of an energy crisis. How would he or she allocate these limited resources over a given time period? Who would determine which regions of the country would get these supplies? Which industries would receive the greatest amounts of resources? What would be the social and political effects of such a crisis? Would new laws be needed to cope with this type of emergency? These problems could be programmed into a computer and the results measured against a real-life situation.

Projecting future problem areas is an important part of the environmentalist's role. Where are energy sources alternative to oil? How effective can fuel conservation be? Does solar energy provide enough heat generation for an average family? These situations can be studied in computer simulations and policies formulated according to their outcomes.

To test your own energy efficiency you might develop your own computer program that looks at the way your family car uses gasoline. Variables such as how much you drive, how fast you drive, and when you drive might all figure into this type of problem. You could then make comparisons with other members of your family and with your friends.

You might also examine questions concerning "over-usage" of the car. Do you ride when you could walk? What effect does this have on your fuel bill, and what effect might it have on our overall energy supply?

As with other social scientists, ecologists and those who study the environment have turned to the computer to store, relay, manipulate, and transfer collected information.

# 8

# How You Can
# Use Computers in the
# Social Studies

The computer's ability to retrieve, store, and index information is one of the primary tools of the social scientist. This tool can also be available to you, if you learn how to use computer reference services.

## USING DATA BASES

Within the past ten years most university and public libraries have become part of nationwide computer reference services called data bases. Using computers these services compile information on subjects that have been treated in books, and in magazine and newspaper articles. The subject areas covered include the following: the physical and biological sciences, medicine, agriculture, engineering, business, government, history, political science, psychology, education, language, literature, music, art, and home economics. The services can provide a printed list of books, magazine articles, and speeches based on your subject needs, with complete bibliographic citations and, in some cases, abstracts or copies of the articles.

For example, suppose you were writing a research paper on George Washington. The procedure for starting a computer search is very easy. First, you as the user must decide what kinds of information you want. Do you want to know where he was born, or facts about his presidency or his job as a general? Second, you will probably have to make an appointment with a search, or information, analyst. This analyst will ask you a series of questions, such as:

1. What is the nature of your project?
2. What subject or subjects will your project cover?
3. What key words best describe your project?

In this case the analyst will try to combine terms and concepts in various ways to find the most relevant citations such as "Washington, president and general." Limits, such as dates or languages, may be imposed on the search as well.

Computerized searches offer many advantages, and in some cases they turn up citations which would have been almost impossible to uncover through the printed indexes. However, computerized data bases, for the most part, cover the most recent years (ten to fifteen years back), while their printed counterparts include earlier years. So the information you get about Washington may be items written in only the past ten or so years. Also, a printed index will serve very well if you find a single subject heading covers your topic. Reference librarians, or systems analysts, are skilled in helping you determinine the best strategy for your topic, whether this be computerized data bases, printed indexes, or a combination.

Most reference centers charge the user for these computerized services. The charges vary according to the amount of computer time used and the number of citations printed. A typical search may cost between ten and twenty dollars.

# EXAMPLE OF A
# SOCIAL SCIENCE DATA BASE

Although there are a variety of data bases available, several concentrate on topics of interest to social scientists and those who may be seeking information on the social sciences. One data base that you might use is the *National Newspaper Index*, which indexes articles from the *Christian Science Monitor*, *The New York Times*, and the *Wall Street Journal*. For students seeking general information or beginning a research project, it can provide current information. It dates from January, 1979, and is updated monthly. Specific topics it covers include:

| | |
|---|---|
| General Interest News | Performing Arts, |
| Business | Literature |
| Life and Living | Social Affairs |
| Leisure-Time Activities | Science, Technology, |
| Home-Centered Arts | and Agriculture |
| Sports, Recreation, | Consumer-Product |
| Travel | Evaluation |
| Environmental Issues | Regional News |

If you wanted to use this index you would go to a library and first ask the reference librarian if it was available. Assuming that it was, you would then tell the librarian your subject, say, for example, baseball. Next, you would have to become more specific and begin to tell the librarian exactly what it was you wanted to find out. In this search you might want to know which team each of these newspapers predicted to win the National League Pennant in 1982. Since most predictions about baseball are printed before the season begins, you would have to tell the librarian dates that these might have been printed. The computer would then search these papers on the given dates for the chosen topic. You would receive a copy of the results of this search.

Another useful data base is *America: History and Life (AHL)*, which covers U.S. and Canadian history, area studies, and current affairs. It is divided into three parts: Article Abstracts and Citations, Index to Book Reviews, and American History Bibliography. This service abstracts entries from nineteen hundred international journals in the social sciences. It is updated three times a year and starts from 1964. Specific emphasis is placed on the following subject areas:

| | |
|---|---|
| American Studies | Local History |
| Cultural History | Military History |
| Economic History | Oral History |
| Ethnic Studies | Prehistory |
| Family History and | Politics and Government |
|    Women's Studies | Popular Culture |
| Folklore | Religious History |
| History | Science, Technology |
| History of Ideas |    and Medicine |
| Historiography and |    (History of) |
|    Methodology | Teaching of History |
| International Relations | Urban Affairs |

You would use this data base in a manner similar to the previous one.


## USING SOCIAL STUDIES
## COMPUTER PROGRAMS

There are many social studies programs available for use on classroom computers. Most of these simulate, or attempt to duplicate, real-life situations. These programs are very useful as they allow you, as the user, to become part of the social studies decision-making process.

One of the most popular of such programs is a simulation exercise called "Oregon Trail." Distributed by the

*There are many social studies programs*
*you can use on a classroom computer that give*
*you an opportunity to participate in simulations*
*of real decision-making situations.*

Minnesota Educational Computing Consortium, this simulation places you in a wagon train headed west to Oregon in the mid-nineteenth century. You have to decide how much money to spend on provisions, when to stop for food, and when to fight Indians and desperadoes. The object of the game is to get to Oregon "in one piece" before winter sets in and you freeze in the mountains.

Other games produced by MECC for social studies classes include "NOMAD" and "Fur Trader." As with "Oregon Trail," you, the student, must make decisions based on data the computer has provided for you. By using these games you will become familiar with the computer and how it can tell you instantly how your decision may affect the outcome of your game.

## USING A WORD PROCESSOR

Another way a computer can be useful to you is through its word processing services. A word processor allows the computer user to move parts or sections of text, make connections with other material, move paragraphs around, and make personalized letters. The user can make changes or corrections even after a printed copy has been made because the computer stores the information until it is erased. For instance, you might write a letter to a friend and want to change a part of it after you have written it. A word processor allows you to do this more quickly and easily than you could on a typewriter. Most word-processing programs have the following standard features:

1. *Dictionary*—checks words in your document against a list of currently spelled words. These lists, depending on the word processing system, range from 10,000 to 45,000 words.

2. *Search and Replace*—finds words or characters in the document and allows you to change a particular word throughout the document.

3. *Overtyping*—enables you to correct errors by striking over a letter.

4. *Global Search*—this will find anything throughout the document.

5. *Centering*—centers a word or groups of words.

6. *Pagination*—prints page number where you want it—top, bottom, left, or right side of the paper.

7. *Screen Oriented*—displays on screen what you will receive when document is actually printed. Allows you to make instantaneous changes.

All popular microcomputers offer word-processing programs. Many companies purchase these word processors for use in their offices.

This chapter has shown you how you might currently use computers in solving, or dealing with, social science problems. The next chapter will discuss the future and how computers may affect your lifestyle in the next twenty years.

# 9

# Computers
# and the Future

The following selection might be part of a book on
United States history in the year 2025. It traces the
development of technology and education in this
country in the latter part of the twentieth century.

## THE EARLY 1980s

As the 1980s began, the use of computers grew at a phe-
nomenal rate. With ever-increasing memory chip capabilities and decreasing size, the amount of storage on one
chip (about the size of a penny) continued to double
every fifteen months. As the memory increased, the cost
of production decreased at a record rate. By 1983, small
microcomputer units were available for below one
hundred fifty dollars.

Schools, businesses, and industries, at all levels, set
up computer/communications laboratories. Through
both federal and state aid, money for these became available to many who could not afford them. Many university teacher-training programs began to require courses in
the use of computer technology in the classroom.

Along with the decreased costs, came several technological breakthroughs. Most notable was the develop-

[70]

ment of a cheap audio visual diskette to use with micro-computers. These diskettes allowed students to see and hear demonstrations while working at computer terminals. As the diskette was being developed, a computer-television set was tested. This device allowed for a switch to be installed on home TV's to link them to major computer facilities.

Eventually, through the use of telephone lines and cable television, these items, along with video tape machines, became standard TV equipment and allowed people to participate in continuing education classes at their leisure. Universities, many large school systems, and private industry began to use this technology as part of their educational programs. Eventually, interactive education programs were available on a daily basis. The cost was tied to cable rental. Linkage to satellite communications made international programming available as well. Students could enroll in a course at universities in Paris, London, and their own state, all at the same time. Examinations were given through the computer and records kept at the United Nations' education headquarters in New York.

To handle the increased use of computers and other high-technology equipment in schools, the federal government established an Office of Technology within the Department of Education. One of the many proposals made to this office was to set up learning centers in non-traditional school settings such as shopping malls and recreation centers so that people with limited time and funds could participate in remedial as well as enrichment education programs.

## THE LATE 1980s

An Internationl Education Data Bank was started through the cooperation of the United Nations and the

UN Economic and Social Council (UNESCO). The contributors to this project collected and disseminated technological and scientific data. Additionally the agency collected information on ways that various countries were using telecommunications and computers in their school systems. Third World countries were particularly interested in this project as they saw it as a mechanism by which their countries could gather technological information at a low cost.

Toward the end of the decade, problems with software development still plagued users of micro- and minitelecommunications systems. Despite technological breakthroughs, large-scale technological curriculum projects had only just begun in 1985. Many users relied on materials that were eight and ten years old. The National Computer Curriculum Project was organized to augment the software developed by private industry. Areas that were considered to be of prime importance were reading, mathematics, science, and second language usage. In five years, the project produced well over fifteen thousand lessons for elemementary and secondary students.

## THE 1990s
## TO EARLY 2000s

Under the 1990 edition of the Education Act, every person in the United States was entitled to have a computer. Another part of this act established a national education data collection service that would be available to all schools. This reference-retrieval system was also tied into the National Public Broadcasting Center and fed to all homes, free of charge.

Libraries were now completely computerized and automated. They were tied to regional, state, and national information systems. If a book or journal was not available locally, a national search was made. Once the document or book was located, an instant copy was made and sent out to the borrower. Costs for these systems were paid on a subscription basis.

Three national television channels began to devote programming exclusively to educational-technological subjects on a twenty-four-hour basis. Programs from preschool through adult continuing education were offered. Credit was given by the newly established National University of the Air, and one could obtain a college degree through the use of a computer.

The size of memory chips decreased as their capabilities increased. The entire 1990 census data could be stored on one memory chip half the size of a penny. Costs also continued to decline, to the point where anyone could grow his or her own silicon chip at home with the aid of a hobby kit.

Teachers' groups began to lobby against the increased use of communication technology as some were being displaced by their increased use. As part of the National Teacher's Training Act of 1995, the federal government promised to retrain and place all teachers who lost their jobs due to technology. Most teachers became computer facilitators and were quickly hired by private industry. Another part of this act required all those who were going to work in educational settings to be trained in the use and repair of educational and communications equipment.

Since many nations were now tied into the UN's education data bank, an International Education Conference on the establishment of a multinational computer language was called in 1999. This conference developed the first truly international language, which was to be incorporated into all educational programs worldwide. Nations who participated agreed to require knowledge of this language as part of the degree requirements for secondary education graduation beginning in 2005.

The International University held its first commencement exercises in 2010. Graduates included those from 195 different countries. The school had no buildings, no campus, no football team. It functioned out of six telecomputer centers in Houston, Tokyo, Moscow, Paris, Sydney, and São Paulo. None of its students had paid to attend; each country provided the equipment and financial support needed.

The Select Privacy Act of 2000 required that everyone obtain a special security code for their own personal accounts. This was done to stop the rise in electronic-computer crime. The banking industry was especially eager for this bill to become law as millions of dollars had been taken from their accounts in what was called "the Great Electronic Switch of 2000."

As you read this scenario, did any of the ideas seem far out, or do you think that the computer and its parallel technological developments will have any even greater effect on society? How will computers affect the public's right to information access and the individual's right to privacy?

## INFORMATION, PRIVACY, AND COMPUTERS

For the most part, the scenario was positive, stressing how technology might help expand and enrich our education systems. If we are not careful, however, we can use these same technological tools to harm and abuse others, especially in the area of accessing information, which poses a threat to the right to privacy.

Most people don't realize the amount and type of information that are collected about each of us from birth until we die. For example, right at the start of life, our births are recorded by state and local officials. Information on these birth certificates includes names of mother and father, and their address, blood type, and countries of origin. Our school records include all the grades we made in our classes, times absent, present, and tardy. If we wish to work, we need to obtain a Social Security card. This establishes a Social Security account in which the names of our employers are recorded along with how much we've made. When we put a telephone in our home, a record of whom we call is started. Taking college entrance tests also puts our name and scores in a vast data bank as well. Should we open a savings or checking account, this information is stored and recorded. Joining the armed services also establishes more records and information about us. All this information is stored in large computer banks across the nation.

While most of this information, if released to others, would not harm us, it is personal data about each of us. The Privacy Act of 1974 "permits an individual to have access to records containing personal information on them kept by Federal Agencies. . . ." While this act helps individuals at the federal level, it does not protect them against those who might gather information from large computer data banks without their permission. These people could be gathering information about our spending habits, where we live or what our driving habits are.

This can occur, unknowingly, to any individual. Consider that when someone applies for a credit card in a department store or to an oil company, a computer search is made to check the applicant's credit rating. Should there be one mistake, or human error, credit may be denied.

What can we do to stop information abuse and misuse? Several ideas have been proposed:

1. Make a national law that would protect individuals from misuse of their records by others.

*Computer literacy—the ability to use computers effectively—will be necessary for almost all occupations in the future.*

2. Make stealing, by electronic or computer means, a crime punishable by long jail sentences.
3. Not allow companies or governments to make national computer searches without an individual's knowledge and consent.

The amount and quantity of information that is produced and gathered on a daily basis is staggering. If we only look at the number of microcomputers in public schools, estimated at 300,000 units in 1982, and the quantity of data that could be produced by these machines, literally millions of pages, it doesn't take long to realize that control and restraint in the gathering of information is quickly approaching. Rather than relying on laws alone, all persons who work with computers must begin to realize the enormous responsibility they have in protecting the rights of others. Computer files with private information need to be protected and not be interfered with. It is up to each computer user to maintain an ethical posture concerning the proper use of personal information.

## CAREERS IN COMPUTERS AND THE SOCIAL SCIENCES

The United States Bureau of Labor Statistics estimates that by 1990 there will be 685,000 jobs available in the computer field. These will include computer operators, computer programmers, systems analysts, computer technicians, and maintenance personnel. Most of these positions will require some technical training and expertise, but not all occupations related to computers will require engineering or programming capabilities. In fact, most will merely require a basic understanding of computer operations and applications.

Social scientists will need to know how to get information into and out of computers in a fast, reliable manner. For example, copies of most historical records are rapidly being transferred to data banks. While the originals are still being preserved, most historians and archivists, in the future, will need to learn how to use files in computer banks and how to store data they wish to retrieve and manipulate. In essence, they will need to become "computer literate," which means that they will need to learn about and operate certain types of computers.

This will be true not only of historians, but of all who may be engaged in social research. As more and more information is gathered and as more and more sophisticated statistical analysis of data is asked for, computers will take over the "drudge" work of social scientists. For instance, demographers and sociologists who study census data will rely more and more on computers to complete their tasks. Geographers and cartographers will count on computer-enhanced satellite photos to make their jobs easier. Teachers in all subject areas will increasingly use computers to enrich their classrooms by having students use computers to complete lessons, play games, and take tests. Many jobs in government also will require a knowledge of computer operations to record and transfer tax records, death certificates, and even traffic violations. In short, within the next twenty years there will be very few jobs, or occupations, untouched by the computer or the technological revolution.

## PREPARING
## FOR FUTURE TECHNOLOGY

What can you as an average student do to prepare yourself both academically and vocationally for a world that is dominated by technology? The first step in becoming prepared is to take any computer literacy courses your school offers. These classes will give you a working knowledge of computers as well as hands-on experience. Over 300,000 microcomputers were in schools in 1982, as well as thousands of terminals that were tied directly to large computers. Most secondary schools offer at least one and sometimes as many as eight different kinds of classes in this area. They range from basic courses to business data processing and programming classes.

If you are really interested in working with computers, you might also want to spend some time at a computer camp. These camps, held during the summer, train beginners and experts on different kinds of computers. Over the past few years many camps have been organized to provide young people with basic computer literacy and to teach more advanced programming skills. Check with local computer stores or colleges and universities for addresses and phone numbers. One source that publishes lists of these camps is:

Computer Town, USA
People's Computer Company
P.O. Box E
Menlo Park, CA 94025

After you've become computer literate, it's time to buy your own computer! This may sound farfetched, but a beginning computer system could be purchased for under two hundred dollars, or the price of a stereo turntable. After you've decided which computer to purchase (a list of companies that make computers appears on pages 85 and 86), you may want to join a computer club. These clubs bring together people interested in computers and their applications. There are many throughout the country. On the following page, several are listed with their addresses.

Computer Education Resource Coalition (CERC)
Lesley College
29 Everett Street
Cambridge, MA 02238

Computer-Using Educators (CUE)
c/o Don McKell
1776 Education Park Drive
San Jose, CA 95133

Digital Equipment Computer Educational Users
Group
One Iron Way
Marlboro, MA 01752

Northwest Council for Computer Education
Computer Center
Eastern Oregon State College
La Grande, OR 97850

These clubs are for both the beginner and expert computer user. In almost every city a number of local computer clubs have been formed. You can get the names and addresses of these from local computer stores. Usually these clubs meet once a week and discuss computer programs and problems.

Finally, most colleges and universities offer courses in computers and computer science, and most now have basic computer literacy courses for noncomputer science majors. Several colleges are now requiring all of their students to take at least one course in computer literacy no matter what their major. Other colleges are now requiring students to purchase a microcomputer, with the option of selling it back after graduation. It is not unlikely that graduation requirements at most colleges and universities, in the near future will include competency in computers and computer technology.

The people who first began to develop the idea of a computer to ease mathematical computations had no idea that one day a computer would be able to complete thousands of calculations in a few moments. As with these early pioneers, we can't imagine what new inventions may be forthcoming that will change our views about computers even more. The possibilities of computer usage and development are almost limitless, and all of us will benefit from these in our work and lifestyle. Social scientists will be part of these changes using computers in their work to help benefit society.

# Appendix

*Howard H. Aiken*—inventor of Automatic Sequence Controlled Calculator called Mark I. Began operation in 1944. Was able to perform three additions every second. Obsolete by 1959.

*Charles Babbage*—English inventor and mathematician (1792–1871). Attempted to build steam-driven calculating device, the difference engine, that would compute mathematical tables such as logarithms. Machine was to be similar to modern calculator, with memory and print space. Never completed due to technical difficulties.

*John Bardeen, Walter H. Brattain, and William Schockley*—inventors of first transistor (1947). Enabled computers to move away from vacuum-tube technology to smaller, less costly units.

*George Boole*—developed algebraic logic (eighteenth century) that was later used in computer logic systems.

*J. Presper Eckert and John W. Mauchly*—designers of first electronic computer ENIAC (*E*lectronic *N*umerical *I*ntegrator *A*nd *C*alculator)) at University of Pennsylvania in 1946.

*Herman Hollerith* (1860–1929)—inventor of the Hollerith Tabulating Machine. This machine was used in the 1890 United States Census, which was the first large-scale application of tabulating machinery. The machine processed data, mostly numbers, through the use of a punched card, much as data is fed into modern computers.

*Joseph-Marie Jacquard*—invented an automated loom (weaving device) that used punched paper cards to reproduce designs (1801).

*John Kemery and Thomas Kurtz*—developers of BASIC (*B*eginners *A*ll-Purpose *S*ymbolic *I*nstruction *C*ode) computer language (1963) at Dartmouth College.

*Gottfried Wilhelm Leibniz* (1696–1716)—extended Pascal's calculator to multiply, divide, and calculate numerical roots. Also developed a step-wheel calculator (hand-held device).

*John Napier* (1550–1617)—inventor of logarithms, and mechanical device for simple mathematical operations called Napier's Rods or Bones.

*William Oughtred* (1575–1660)—developer of the slide rule. Achieved by placing two of Napier's logarithms on an ordered scale.

*D. D. Parmallee*—invented key-driven adding machine (eighteenth century).

*Blaise Pascal* (1623-1662)—at eighteen produced a machine that could add and subtract digits and included principle of "adding wheel." Still used in car mileage indicators.

*George Scheutz* (1785–1873)—created calculator that could carry results to fourteen places and print out results.

# For Further
# Information

## ASSOCIATIONS

The following organizations are involved in furthering interest in computers. Both publish journals and/or newsletters. They encourage student participation and may have special membership rates for students.

Association for Educational Communications
and Technology (AECT)
1126 Sixteenth St., N.W.
Washington, DC 20036

Association for Computing Machinery
1122 Avenue of the Americas
New York, NY 10036

## SOFTWARE CATALOGS
## AND REVIEWS

The following is a list of software catalogs and journals that list current software. All include social studies materials.

Creative Discount Software
256 S. Robertson, Suite 2156
Beverly Hills, CA 90211

Curriculum Product Review
530 University Avenue
Palo Alto, CA 94301

K-12 Micro Media
172 Broadway
Woodcliff Lake, NJ 07675

Minnesota Educational Computing Consortium
2520 Broadway Drive
St. Paul, MN 55113


## COMPUTER MANUFACTURERS

The following is a partial list of hardware manufacturers. Names of the computers are included with the addresses.

| | |
|---|---|
| Apple Computer, Inc.<br>10260 Bandley Drive<br>Cupertino, CA 95014 | Apple II, Apple II E<br>Apple III, Lisa |
| Atari, Inc.<br>1265 Borregas Avenue<br>Sunnyvale, CA 94086 | Atari 400, Atari 800,<br>Atari 1200 |
| Commodore Business<br>Machines, Inc.<br>950 Rittenhouse Road<br>Morristown, PA 19403 | Commodore-Pet,<br>Vic-20 Vic-64 |
| Heath/Zenith<br>Benton Harbor, MI<br>49022 | Heath-Kits |

| | |
|---|---|
| International Business Machines (IBM)<br>P.O. Box 328<br>Boca Raton, FL 33432 | IBM-P.C. |
| Radio Shack<br>400 Atrium<br>1 Tandy Center<br>Fort Worth, TX 76102 | TRS-80 Model I, II, or III |
| Sinclair Research Limited<br>50 Stanford Street<br>Boston, MA 02114 | Sinclair ZX-81 |
| Texas Instruments, Inc.<br>P.O. Box 10508<br>Lubbock, TX 79408 | TI (various models) |

# For Further Reading

## BOOKS

KAREN BILLINGS AND DAVID MOURSAND. *Are You Computer Literate?* Beaverton, OR: dilithium Press, 1979. Tells what you need to know to run a computer.

CHRISTOPHER EVANS. *The Micro-Millennium.* New York: Viking Press, 1979. History of Computers and Their Future.

CARIN E. HORN AND JAMES L. POIROT. *Computer Literacy—Problem Solving with Computers.* Austin, TX: Sterling Swift, 1981.

SUSAN D. LIPSCOMB AND MARGARET A. ZUANICH. *Basic Fun—Computer Games, Puzzles and Problems Children Can Write.* New York: Avon Books, 1982. Computer games in BASIC Language.

ARTHUR LUERHMAN, HERBERT PECKHAM, AND MARTHA RAMIREZ. *First Course in Computing.* New York: McGraw-Hill, 1982.

LINDA MALONE AND JERRY JOHNSON. *BASIC Discoveries.* Palo Alto, CA: Creative Publications, 1981. Computer programs in BASIC language.

JERRY WILLIS AND WILLIAM DONELY, JR. *Nailing Jelly to a Tree*. Beaverton, OR: dilithium Press, 1981. Using a computer for a beginner.

## MAGAZINES

*BYTE*. 70 Main Street, Peterborough, NH 03458

*Creative Computing*. P.O. Box 789-M, Morristown, NJ 07960

*Educational Technology*. 140 Sylvan Avenue, Englewood Cliffs, NJ 07632

*Electronic Learning*. Scholastic Inc., 902 Sylvan Avenue, Box 2001, Englewood Cliffs, NJ 07632.

*Personal Computing*. P.O. Box 1408, Riverton, NJ 08077

*Popular Computing*. 70 Main Street, Peterborough, NH 03458

## SELECTED MAGAZINE ARTICLES

"And Man Created the Chip," *Newsweek*, June 30, 1980.

"Technology and Social Studies," *Social Education*, May 1983.

"The Chip," *National Geographic*, October 1982.

# Index